# Wandering Woman: Arizona

The Ultimate Road Trip: One Woman's
Journey Across the United States by Car

Julie Bettendorf

# Contents

# Introduction

## "Not all who wander are lost."

*Are you sure?* I thought to myself, as I tried not to panic. I was a long way from anything familiar, but that was how it should be. I had driven thousands of miles on dusty, pothole-filled roads. It's often on the worst roads that you can discover something truly amazing.

My dusty CRV was parked beside me, containing one restless dog and a variety of snack bags, all empty by now. There were no buildings in sight, no cars or people or movement at all. Only the constant humming of the insects as they buzzed around my head.

I turned to my left – another straight road that trailed off into the distance. I glanced over to the right, then behind me – two more barely discernible roads stretched out into the abyss. I was in a four-way intersection with no signs, no sense of direction, and no sign of life for several miles. No cell service either, and that meant no GPS. *Damn*, I thought. *I'm lost.*

*How did I get here?* I couldn't help but feel like this little intersection was a cruel metaphor for life. I began to daydream, imagining each road might transport me back to a different time, a different role in my life, and a different me.

If I took the road from whence I came, it could lead me all the way back to Oregon, back to my cheating third husband, back to a life of loneliness and solitude. There is no greater loneliness than being married to someone who isn't actually present in your life.

If I took the road to my left, perhaps it could take me back to my career as a dental hygienist, a job I hated deep down in my soul. There is something so disengaging about cleaning teeth for a living. It's a disgusting, smelly way to get a paycheck. It pays well, which is great, but the best part is the huge gob of friends I enjoy to this day.

Or maybe the road to my right, *yes – maybe that's the path*, I imagined. Maybe it could take me back to my real treasure, my kids. Back to their smiling, innocent faces as toddlers, as they danced around the Christmas tree and their father and I were still married. Back when they still needed me for every little thing.

But, that was just it. I didn't feel needed anymore. My kids weren't toddlers anymore – they were both full-grown adults, and far too busy for me. My dental buddies were still working, but I wasn't. Dental hygiene had robbed me of the cartilage in my fingers, giving me severe, disabling arthritis. And, I wouldn't be returning to any more husbands either, because three marriages were quite enough for me.

All three of these paths, all three of these roles – the wife, the mother, and the dental hygienist – had seemingly been stripped from me within a year. I was lost and looking to find myself again.

The funny thing about this phrase, "not all who wander are lost" – is that, in my experience, wandering and being lost walk hand-in-hand with one another, and the expression can be flipped. In my experience, not all who are lost are wandering, and that is a real disservice to the beauty and clarity that the world has to offer.

When one becomes lost, wandering is the only option to guide oneself back to a path. After all, one could not come upon any dirt path at all without wandering.

I began wandering at an early age, both with my mind and with my feet. At eight years old, I was reading a book about archaeology and dreaming of one day seeing Egypt. I didn't follow a traditional path in high school either, going heavily into foreign languages, in hopes of one day using them.

At twenty-five years old, I divorced my first husband (the dental student who talked me into becoming a dental hygienist so I could work for him) and decided to give traveling a real shot. I took off for the Andes and Macchu Picchu, climbing up ancient Inca stone steps to reach the magnificent ruins.

Anyone who has been to Macchu Picchu will tell you there is something ethereal and deeply spiritual about the place. The ruins stretch out across the emerald green mountains, way up in the middle of the sky. Macchu Picchu gave me my first experience of feeling history. This trip inspired me to come back and complete a degree in archaeology, and I've been wandering ever since.

More travel followed including a backpack trip around Europe for three months, by myself, and trips to Britain, Italy, and Greece. I visited the burial places of Crusaders, mummies, and ancient kings. I happened upon the castle of my namesake in Bettendorf, Luxembourg, and wandered my way through European history.

My favorite excursion by far was finally seeing Egypt with my daughter in 2012. Just like my childhood dream envisioned, I rode a camel beneath the pyramids of Giza, with my head wrapped in some man's sweaty turban. It was perfect.

Traveling has always been my own personal antidote to pain. I went to Mexico after my first and second divorces, Canada after my third, and Italy after my dad died. Call it avoidance if you want, but I call it an accelerated form of healing in the purest sense of the word. I believe travel can heal your soul.

Wandering has always worked its wonders on me – made me feel renewed, rejoiceful, grateful, and purposeful. It's been my medicine.

So, as I stood in that intersection, I once again wondered how wandering had led me so astray this time. *What the hell am I supposed to do now?* It was then that I realized that one last path had not been considered yet – the path which stretched straight out in front of me. *Which role does this represent?* I pondered.

The answer smacked me in the face.

That last dirt road – the only path that could take me where I wanted to go, the only path that ever truly healed me or showed me the way – was the path of the traveler. The wife, the mother, and the hygienist roles – though valued in their time – were sitting in the bleachers now. It was time to welcome and enable my boldest, bravest, and perhaps most pivotal role yet:

The role of the Wandering Woman.

# Welcome to Wandering Woman

This book is for you – the grieving empty nester mom, the begrudged housewife, the woman in need of a drastic change in her life. Really, this book is for anyone with a passion for traveling. If you feel lost with no sense of direction or purpose in life, that's a bonus – this book will be even more appealing to you. And lastly, if you're a man reading this book, congratulations for holding a book with the word woman in the title. You're contributing to gender equality, and that's pretty neat.

I decided to combine three of my dearest loves – travel, history, and archaeology – and put them into a book because I believe wandering has the power to change your life. I have been to many areas of the world and had too many outstanding experiences to list. However, by the time both my children had moved out in 2017, I had

Me

never seen my own country – America. It was the perfect time to explore a new country (my own) and discover a new me at the same time.

So, I packed up my Honda CRV, along with some gear and my 14-year-old furry friend, Sadie. Wandering Woman is the chronicle of my journey across eleven states, discovering the joy of getting lost and finding myself along the way.

# Why America?

*A* *merica, the beautiful?* I sure think so, but I didn't realize just how beautiful our country is until I embarked on traveling across eleven western states in a year.

The United States offers everything for the discerning palate. From spectacular beaches, austere mountains, to rolling plains, our country has it all. It's difficult to comprehend just how large and impressive our scenery is, until you experience it first-hand, with the ultimate road trip.

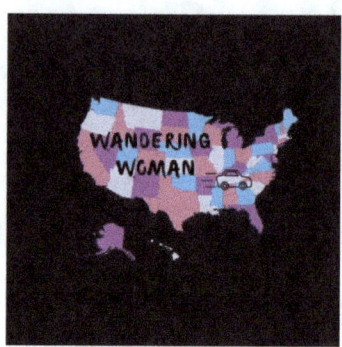

I also realized just how much of our history is missing from U.S. history I was taught as a kid. The history of our country didn't begin with the pilgrims landing on Plymouth Rock in the 1600s. Our history is far more ancient, with rock art and archaeological sites dating back over 12,000 years.

We also owe a tremendous debt to early pioneers who tamed our land. The Mormons and other groups ventured into the great unknown with their families and their worldly possessions. Some of them pulled cumbersome handcarts across the country to settle in inhospitable, dangerous locations.

The goal of Wandering Woman is to bring history back to life and make it interesting again. I am presenting some famous sites, and many little-known ones. You will take the road-less-traveled with me, while we explore ghost towns, rock art sites, archaeological sites, and museums, to discover the colorful tapestry that is our country.

I present some history, including dates, but my goal is to present more of the real-life stories of history, including ghost stories, profiles in history, voices from the past, and moments in time, to give you, the reader, a deeper understanding of the context of history.

This is by no means an exhaustive list of places to visit. In fact, I encourage you to discover America for yourself, as I did, by making a trek across the land by car. You can explore as the early explorers did, just a little more comfortably, with a lot less hardship.

I hope you enjoy this book and take a little time out to discover our beautiful country, and maybe even discover yourself in the process.

Safe Travels,

*Julie Bettendorf*

# Welcome to Arizona

## The Grand Canyon State

Arizona, what's not to love? It's no coincidence it's a hot spot for retirees. The weather is wonderful and the scenery is spectacular with the mighty saguaro cacti reaching up to the sky like silent sentinels protecting the desert and all who live there. You may fall in love with Arizona and its history, with the many rock art sites and searching for treasure in the Superstition Mountains.

## *5 things to love about Arizona:*

The imposing Saguaro cacti

The spectacular Apache Trail through Superstition Mountains

Ancient archaeological sites like painted rocks and Besh Ba Gowah

Historic Tombstone and nearby Fairbank ghost town

San Xavier del Bac and Tumacacori Spanish Missions

# Dreams of Arizona

"*The Arizona desert takes hold of a man's mind and shakes it.*" – **David W. Toll**

"*Well, the trip from then on across Arizona and east of Los Angeles was just one Oasis after another. You can just throw anything out and it will grow there. I like Arizona.*" – **Will Rogers**

"*Arizona is a magnificent state. With something for everyone. I realize that no poem, song, picture, or words could ever do justice to Arizona.*" – **Rick Harris**

# Top Stuff to See in Arizona

### *Favorite Arizona Historical Sites:*

- Tombstone

- Fairbank

### *Favorite Arizona Archaeological Sites:*

- Canyon de Chelley

- Navajo National Monument

### *Favorite Arizona Scenic Drives:*

- Apache Trail through the Superstition Mountains

-

Pinery Canyon Road through the Chiricahua Mountains

### *Favorite Arizona Museums:*

- Musical Instrument Museum, Phoenix

- Superstition Mountain Museum, Apache Trail

### *When driving through Arizona, be on the lookout for:*

- Wild horses and burros, often in the middle of the road.

# Early Arizona

Early Travel into the Superstition Mountains

Early Jerome

Early Bisbee

# Northwestern Arizona

# Grand Canyon

T he ***Grand Canyon*** is truly spectacular. There are many ways to tour
the Grand Canyon, from hiking on foot, to horseback, jeep, and my

favorite, via helicopter. I highly recommend the helicopter version. It's a bit on the spendy side, but the enjoyment of this vast geological wonder is well worth the price.

Human habitation of the Grand Canyon can be traced back to at least 10,500 years ago. At least 4000 years ago, early Native American cultures including Ancestral Puebloan peoples lived in caves along the cliffs.

European exploration into the Grand Canyon began with the Spanish in September 1540, when a group of soldiers from the Coronado expedition came searching for the Seven Cities of Gold. Due to the difficult terrain and inability to access the river, the Spanish didn't return for another two hundred years.

In 1776, two Spanish priests, Dominquez and Escalante, came through the canyon on their way to find a route from Sante Fe, New Mexico, to Monterey, California.

Other explorers followed, including John Wesley Powell, who mapped and catalogued archaeological sites, geological formations, plants, and animals within the canyon.

Whatever route you take to visit the Grand Canyon, you can't help but be moved by the sheer grandeur and beauty of this magical place.

## *How to get to the Grand Canyon:*

The Grand Canyon is in Northwestern Arizona, close to the Nevada and Utah borders. It has several tourism spots, but the most heavily visited area is the South Rim, which is a 90 minute drive from Flagstaff, Arizona, off Interstate 40. You can also catch a train in Williams, Arizona, which travels through the Grand Canyon. I caught my helicopter ride out of Las Vegas, Nevada.

## *A word about the Dominguez Escalante Expedition:*

Two Franciscan priests named Francisco Atanasio Dominguez, who was 36 years old, and 26 year-old Silvestre Velez de Escalante, planned to leave Santa Fe on July 4, 1776, the same day as the signing of the Declaration of Independence.

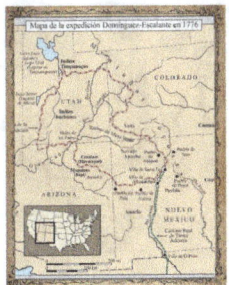

Their goal was to find a route over land from Santa Fe, New Mexico to their mission in Monterey, California. They eventually left Santa Fe on July 29th, traveling over two thousand miles over New Mexico, Colorado, Arizona, and Utah. They never reached Monterey or the Pacific Coast. Crutchfield

# Oatman

*Oatman* began its life in 1904 and grew prosperous from mining gold. Oatman was named for a pioneer family who were attacked and killed by Indians near the area in 1851.

Today it's famous for its burros, which roam the streets. The descendants of today's burros came along with the early prospectors.

The early burros helped in the mines. After the mines closed, the burros ran wild. Town of Oatman

As you stroll the streets of this charming, touristy small town, visit the *1902 Oatman Hotel*, where Clark Gable and Carole Lombard stayed on their wedding night in 1939.

## *How to get to Oatman:*

Oatman is located in northwestern Arizona, off of Route 66, 28 miles from Bullhead City, Arizona.

## *A moment in time:*

The *Oatman massacre* occurred in 1851, when six members of the Oatman family were killed by a group of Tonto-Apache Indians. The Oatman parents and four children were killed. One boy, Lorenzo, was clubbed and left to die.

Two of the Oatman girls, Olive, who was 16, and 10 year-old Mary Ann became captives. Mary Ann died of starvation, and Olive's release was negotiated in 1856. Lorenzo, didn't die. He made his way to friendly Pima Indians, and then to Fort Yuma. He was later reunited with his sister Olive.

Town of Oatman, AZ

## *Voices from the past:*

*"While we tarried here (Mericopa Wells),(sic) Willard and Robert Kelly went down to Oatman's wagon....to bury the dead." from **a letter of Mrs. Wilder to her father, quoted in "The Olive Branch" Sept. 1851.***

*"When I got back I learned my men have returned from their search after the distressed emigrants. They found the wagon diverted over a hundred feet from and two dead bodies, covered over with large stones. One they took to be a man but could not decide about the other. There was nothing of any consequence left in or about the wag-*  *on." **from the journal of Maj. Heintzelman while at Fort Yuma under date of March 8, 1851.***

*"In after years I was passing Oatman Flat with a train, and stopped long enough to gather the bleaching bones and inter them in one grave which was surrounded with pickets." **Mr. Charles Poston, Florence Arizona Enterprise, June 13, 1891.***

# Northeastern Arizona

# Navajo National Monument

*N*avajo National Monument consists of three main groups of cliff dwellings, the **Betatakin**, **Keet Seel**, and **Inscription House**, which was closed when I visited.

Tree-ring dating, known as (Dendrochronology) has identified a major prolonged drought that lasted twenty years, and didn't end until 1300 AD. This drought is believed to be a main reason why the Ancestral Puebloans left the area. Noble, NPS

Betatakin is a Navajo term meaning "ledge house." The spectacular Betatakin ruins were constructed about 1250 AD and contained at least 135 rooms, housing between 100 and 125 people. You can view the Betatakin ruins from afar, but to see them up close you must take one of the ranger-led hikes.

The Keet Seel ruins have 155 rooms and 6 kivas, or ceremonial centers. Tree-ring dating has established the area was settled about 950 AD. There is a wonderful reconstructed kiva at Keet Seel, giving you an idea of the importance of the ceremonial center.

As you walk among the ruins, note the "T" shaped doorways opening onto the plaza.

Both the doorways and the corner windows are rare architectural features in structures of the ancient Southwest.

The Navajo National Monument has a wonderful ***museum***, superbly curated with an amazing collection of artifacts including an original 800 year-old ladder from the cliff dwellings, a turkey-feather belt, dazzling black on white pottery, jewelry, sandals, and other artifacts found during excavations in the area.

## *How to get to Navajo National Monument:*

Navajo National Monument is in northeastern Arizona, about 50 miles from Tuba City, off of Route 160.

## *A word about kivas:*

The word **"*kiva*"** means cellar or underground house, and it was a special place of ceremony. Kivas were used primarily by men, but women and children could enter them for certain ceremonies and at certain times.

When an area was abandoned, kivas were often ritually closed by being filled in and sealed, and the roofs were burned. The photo above, is of a reconstructed kiva at Keet Seel, Navajo National Monument.

# Canyon de Chelley

*C**anyon de Chelley*** (pronounced de-Shay) is a sprawling site containing many archaeological features, including some amazing cliff

dwellings. There are two drives around the rim of the canyon, each with its own spectacular scenery and ancient dwellings.

The area has been home to people for at least 5000 years, including archaic hunter-gatherers, basketmaker culture, ancestral Puebloan, Hopi, and Navajo. Noble, NPS

You can hike down to a ruin known as the White House. It's the only hike you may take by yourself. All other hikes into the ruins are by way of guided tours. You can also hire a guide and use your own vehicle, or take a trip on horseback. Watch out for roaming livestock, especially large cows, which I almost plowed into.

## *How to get to Canyon de Chelley:*

Canyon de Chelley National Monument is in northeastern Arizona, near the town of Chinle, off of Route 191.

## *A word about what happened:*

What happened to these ancient cultures which caused them to abandon their monumental buildings?

• The Mimbres culture disappeared around 1130 AD

• Chaco Canyon, North Black Mesa, and Ancestral Puebloan all disappeared middle to late 1100's

• Mesa Verde and Kayenta cultures disappeared around 1300 AD

• Mogollon culture disappeared around 1400 AD

• Hohokam disappeared late into the 1400's

It was probably a combination of factors that caused the residents to abandon their homes. One of the main causes was a major multi-year drought beginning around 1130 AD. Cultures were impacted differently by this, depending on whether they lived in an area with more or less rainfall. Those that lived at higher elevations with more rainfall tended to cope with the drought better.

Cultures with larger populations like Chaco Canyon, exhausted their food supply more quickly, resulting in conflict over food, land, and other resources. There is some evidence of cannibalism, because human muscle protein has been found in the dried fecal material of ancient humans. Major conflict was inevitable, and it is widely believed that ancient survivors were absorbed into other cultures like the Zuni. [Diamond]

# Homolovi

*T**he Homolovi Ruins** date from 1200 to the late1300s, and were inhabited by the descendants of the Hopi, known as the Hisat'Sinom.

Homolovi I was flooded in the late 1300s by the Little Colorado River nearby.

The people moved to the upper mesas and established Homolovi II, a complex containing between 1200 and 2000 rooms, housing 750 to 1000 people. Arizona State Parks and Trails, Noble

The word Homolovi means "place of the little hills." As you walk along, you can see pottery shards of all colors, shapes, and sizes lying all over the ground. Please don't remove them, because it's illegal.

Near the Homolovi ruins there is also a pioneer cemetery where members of early Mormon pioneer families are buried. In 1876, a small group of Mormon pioneers came to this area and built Sunset Fort. Sunset Fort was later abandoned in 1887 due to droughts and flooding. This small cemetery is named Sunset Cemetery

and it contains just a few graves of young children, the youngest a mere 2 months old, and the oldest just under 9 years old.

## *How to get to Homolovi:*

The Homolovi ruins are 3 miles northeast of Winslow, Arizona off of Hwy 87. As you drive out to Homolovi, watch out for wild burros along the road.

# Winslow

***W**inslow* is the site of the ***Meteor Crater***. When you see the Meteor Crater on a map of Arizona, it's easy to overlook it, but don't. You may be wondering what it is doing in a history travel book. The truth is, the meteor smacking into the earth *is* history. It happened about 50,000 years ago.

The meteor is estimated to have measured about 150 feet across and weighed hundreds of thousands of tons. It traveled at a mind-boggling 26,000 miles per hour and slammed into the earth with a strength greater than 20 million tons of TNT.

The meteor left a crater behind that is 700 feet deep and 4000 feet across. Photographs do not begin to show how massive the crater is. I took 7 photos to capture it all. The crater was first recorded in 1871 by one of General Custer's scouts, named Franklin, who named the crater Franklin's hole.
Meteor Crater Enterprises

Visiting the Meteor Crater is a spectacular experience, because nothing can quite prepare you for the sheer size of it. The Meteor Crater is the star, but the site also has a museum which contains a nicely presented collection of meteors, historical photographs, space exploration information, and NASA paraphernalia, including an Apollo test capsule.

## *How to get to Winslow:*

Winslow is off of Arizona Route 40, 58 miles from Flagstaff.

# Central Arizona

# Walnut Canyon

T o view the cliff dwellings at **Walnut Canyon**, you descend some
meandering, winding stone step trails, which only adds to the mag-

nificence of the place. When I visited, Walnut Canyon had a light dusting of snow on the canyon walls. Spectacular.

The dramatic, tree-lined cliffs of Walnut Canyon, hold several cliff dwellings which were built about 800 years ago, between 1125 and 1250 AD, and lived in by the Sinagua people. Noble, NPS

They are named the Sinagua, which means "without water" because they lived in an arid, inhospitable terrain. In the rocky soil, they grew corn, beans, and squash, by developing terraces to hold water.

They had a varied diet of their crops, along with small animals like rabbits, wild turkeys, and deer.

## *How to get to Walnut Canyon:*

Walnut Canyon National Monument is 7 miles east of Flagstaff, off Interstate 40.

# Palatki

The ***Palatki Complex*** was constructed by the Sinagua people in 1100 AD and used until 1275 AD. Between 40 and 80 people lived there.

Palatki has a wide variety of rock art, including the oldest images, dating from 12,000 years ago up to historical graffiti from the 1900s.

The subjects are diverse, including bear, deer, sheep, and pronghorn antelope used to conjure up hunting magic.

Among the designs are horseman figures dating from 1583 when the Spanish visited the valley.

There is also a design of the moon and Venus, thought to be an image of the supernova which happened in 1054 AD. Palatki is a Hopi word meaning "red house." [Noble]

## *How to get to Palatki:*

The Palatki ruins are 30 minutes west of Sedona, off of Hwy 89A.

## *Profiles in history:*

*Charles Willard* was an early pioneer to the Verde Valley. He established himself in a cave at the Palatki ruins in 1924. Willard made the cave into a simple dwelling containing a bed, a table, and a stove.

He lived in the cave until 1925, at which time he moved into a ranch house nearby. Willard grew a wide variety of fruit trees including peaches, pears, plums, and apples. He also grew yellow watermelons, peanuts, grapes, and blackberries.

# Honanki

The ***Honanki Cliff Dwellings*** were built from 1050 AD to 1300 AD by the Sinagua people. Tree ring dating established one log was cut in 1271 AD. The complex contained about 60 rooms.

Archaeologists found Clovis projectile points in the area which were used by paleo-indians from 11,500 BC to 9,000 BC.

The site has over 2000 pictographs, some of which are from the Archaic period of 9000 BC to 300 AD. [Noble]

The Honanki site was named by an early archaeologist named Fewkes, who excavated the site in 1913. Honanki is a Hopi word meaning "bear house."

## *How to get to Honanki:*

The Honanki ruins are near the Palatki ruins.

# Tuzigoot

You arrive at the ***Tuzigoot*** ruins after walking a short trail 1/3 of a mile long. When you climb to the top of the ruins, you have a spectacular view of the entire valley.

The ruins are the remains of a 110 room ***pueblo*** built between 1000 AD and 1400 AD by the Sinagua people. It is a 2-story complex with very few doors.

The people entered by climbing down ladders through the roof openings. Tuzigoot was named by the workers who reconstructed it. The original name is the Apache word for "crooked water".

Tree ring dating ranges from 1137 AD to 1386 AD. Archaeologists have found spear points in the area that have been dated to 13,000 years ago.
Noble

The *museum* at Tuzigoot has remnants of ancient textiles, pottery, stone tools, stone effigy figures, and wonderful twig animal figures which are 2,000 to 4,000 years old.

## *How to get to Tuzigoot:*

The Tuzigoot ruins are located 52 miles south of Flagstaff, and 90 miles north of Phoenix along Hwy 89A.

# Jerome

**J**erome is a quirky, picturesque little town clinging to a hillside, known
as *Cleopatra Hill*. The town gets its name from Eugene M. Jerome,

president of the United Verde Copper Company, although he never visited the town named after him. The first mining claims were made in 1876, and within 20 years, Jerome was called the "Billion dollar copper camp". During its peak, 15,000 people were crammed into the town, which boasted two dozen saloons. Jerome was called the town that is "Too Strong to Die."
Finch

Jerome has a small, but excellent history *museum* with a fascinating collection of artifacts. The items you will see include an old doctor's bag from the first doctor in Jerome, Dr. Myron Carrier, Chinese opium paraphernalia, and an old dental chair.

The museum also has some interesting mining items including an underground toilet used by the miners, and a stretcher used to transport injured miners up to the surface.

The **Hotel Connor** is one of the many vintage buildings you will see. Built in 1898, the hotel featured a call bell and electricity in each room. A bar and billiard tables filled the downstairs.

As you walk around town, don't forget to see the shell of the **Bartlett Hotel**, built in 1901. It was built on the site of the former wooden Grandview Hotel, built in 1898 and destroyed by fire. Rooms in the Bartlett were each painted a different color and decorated with ornate, expensive furnishings.

The building grew unstable from the shifting ground and slides during the 1930s, and abandoned completely in the 1940s. Sections of the hotel were dismantled and sold off, including the entire top floor.

## *How to get to Jerome:*

Jerome is about 100 miles north of Phoenix along Arizona Route 89A.

# Montezuma's Well

**M**ontezuma's Well is a deep, mysterious, inky, black pool of water which is inhabited by three creatures that eat each other. On the bottom of the food chain is a tiny shrimp-like amphipod, which is eaten by freshwater leeches and water scorpions.

***Cliff dwellings*** are built into the walls of the well. These structures date from the 1100s, and were built by the Sinagua people. They were deserted by 1425 AD. <sup>Noble, NPS</sup>

Other housing structures were built in the area, beginning in 600 AD, including pit houses, rock shelters, and pueblos.

There are also some fine examples of ***historical graffiti*** from the 1890s.

## *How to get to Montezuma's Well:*

Montezuma's Well is 6 miles north of Montezuma's Castle.

# Montezuma's
# Castle

*M*ontezuma's Castle is an easy walk down a gradual path, and it rewards you with a dramatic view of a spectacular structure. The "castle" contains five stories, and has twenty rooms. It was built by the Sinagua, between 1100 AD and 1300 AD. The walls were plastered with mud, and you can still see the handprints of the builders in the walls.

The Hopi called the castle Sakaytaka, which means "place where the step ladders are going up." It received its current name from European Americans who came in the 1800s, although Montezuma was leader of the Aztecs centuries after the "castle" was built.

During archaeological excavations in the 1930s, many burials were found, including one of a woman in her 30s, who was buried with a large amount of beautiful jewelry. Noble, NPS

## *How to get to Montezuma's Castle:*

Montezuma's Castle is located north of Camp Verde, 50 miles south of Flagstaff.

# Fort Apache

***F**ort Apache* was first established in 1870, and now lies within the boundaries of the White Mountain Indian Reservation. It served as a strategic location for soldiers to battle the Apache during the Apache Wars, which ended with the surrender of Geronimo.

The fort has many historical buildings, all in excellent condition. As you walk around the extensive grounds, you can begin with **General Crook's residence** built in 1871. Crook commanded the regiment.

Near the Crook residence, there is a **memorial** dedicated to three privates killed in conflict with Indians in 1881.

You can also visit the reconstructed stone **Captain's quarters**, first built in 1892, the large Victorian **Commanding Officer's quarters**, built in 1892, and the **Junior officer's quarters** built between 1883 and 1888.

You will also notice the massive ***Theodore Roosevelt Indian Boarding School*** across the parade ground. John Welch, Karl Hoerig, Stephen Grede, White Mountain Apache Tribe

## *How to get to Fort Apache:*

Fort Apache is located within the White Mountain Apache Reservation, 4 miles west of the town of Whiteriver, Arizona, along Hwy 73.

# Kinishba

***The Kinishba Ruins*** were built by the Mogollon people around 1250 AD. By 1325 AD, Kinishba had 600 rooms and housed 400-800 people.

Kinishba is a system of plazas, kivas, and individual rooms.

The Southwestern anthropologist and explorer, Adolph Bandelier was the first to record Kinishba in April, 1883.

The ruins are in a stunningly beautiful setting, and you may have them all to yourself, as I did.

As you walk around, notice the stonework, which is very intricate. It's a mosaic of small perfectly cut, reddish blocks of stone, held together by small shards of stone, with no mortar. <sup>Noble</sup>

When you are driving to Kinishba, look out for wild horses, which love to wander into the road.

## *How to get to Kinishba:*

The Kinishba ruins are located within the White Mountain Apache Reservation near Whiteriver, Arizona. You must first go to the Fort Apache Museum and Cultural Center in Fort Apache.

# Phoenix

***T**he **Musical Instrument Museum*** is truly a world-class museum, and a must-see when you are in Phoenix.

It contains a massive, fascinating collection of musical instruments from across the world, and from across the centuries. Finch

The museum also contains **masks**, **costumes**, and other performance and entertainment artifacts.

You will find it amazing, whether you have a passion for music or not.

I began with the top floor, which is geographically organized with instruments from all over the world. The Africa section contains an interesting mask that represents *Elvis Presley.*

There is also an amazing exhibit of instruments made out of ordinary, recycled goods including a banjo made out of a cheese box.

The European section of the museum has bagpipes, harps, and a drum once belonging to the Irish group, the Chieftains.

Don't miss the marvelously intricate **thumb pianos**.

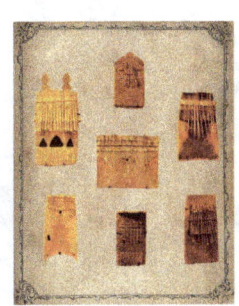

There are musical instruments here which are thousands of years old, but my favorite section of the museum is a collection of self-playing musical instruments, known as **band organs**, many of which are hundreds of years old.

One strikingly beautiful piece is a **musical picture frame** from Switzerland.

As the music plays, the tiny figures move to the music.

The bottom floor belongs to the artists and contains memorabilia and instruments like **Elvis Presley's army uniform, one of Carlos Santana's guitars, Johnny Cash's black suit, and a drum set from the Who.**

## How to get to the Musical Instrument Museum:

The address of the Musical Instrument Museum is 4725 E. Mayo Blvd in Phoenix.

# Tonto National Monument

*Tonto National Monument* lies in a desert which looks inhospitable, but in fact, a group called the Salado lived there. The Salado got their name because of the Rio Salado, or Salt River. The area known as the Tonto Basin was first populated in 100 AD to 600 AD, with a peak population appearing in the 1100s. <sup>Noble, NPS</sup>

The *cliff dwellings* at Tonto are about 700 years old. The Salado spent a lot of time on the roofs of their dwellings and outside, using their houses mainly for sleeping, cooking, storage, and sheltering for the winter. It's a half mile climb uphill to reach the lower cliff dwelling, and a site called the *Annex*.

The lower cliff dwelling once had about 20 rooms, 16 of which were on the ground floor, with several having two stories. The cliff dwelling probably housed between 60 and 70 people. You reach the upper cliff dwelling by taking a three-hour tour led by a park ranger.

There are many signs the Salado left behind in their dwellings including blackened walls from fires lit over 600 years ago, and handprints and finger marks from children and women who plastered the walls of the homes.

When archaeologists excavated at Tonto, they found plant remains including dried beans, yucca sandals, baskets, textiles woven of cotton, yucca, and hair, a 30-inch bow, charms, dice, and many other artifacts. The *museum* contains many of these finds.

## *How to get to Tonto National Monument:*

Tonto National Monument is near Roosevelt, Arizona, about a two hour drive from Phoenix.

# Apache Trail

T he scenery on ***Apache Trail*** is spectacular, with winding, hairpin
turns that take you up into the mountains and huge rock outcrop-

pings. A large section of the road is unpaved, narrow, and sometimes goes down into one lane. It can be a harrowing journey in some places, but well worth the drive. It's beautiful Arizona at its best.

There is a wonderful little museum called the ***Superstition Mountain Museum***, which contains entire walls of ***treasure maps*** of various theories on how to get to the Lost Dutchman Mine.

You will also see ***mining tools, eyeglasses*** and other artifacts from ***Jacob Waltz***, the Dutchman.

There is also a handsome ensemble of **Conquistador armor** which was found in the area.  Superstition Mountain Museum

## *How to get to the Apache Trail:*

The Apache Trail is also known as Arizona State Route 88 and starts at Apache Junction, ending at Theodore Roosevelt Dam.

## *A word about the Lost Dutchman Mine:*

There is a legend that tells of the time when the Jesuits were expelled from the Missions by Spain. The Jesuit priests traveled up into the Superstition Mountains and buried the treasures of the church there.

The Jesuits left a series of carved clues including hearts, a priest figure, and diamond figures carved into Saguaro cacti and onto rocks in the Superstition Mountains.

Many have searched for the treasure, including the Peraltas, a group of Mexican men who ventured into the mountains in 1846. The entire group was massacred by Apache Indians.

The most famous of the treasure hunters was a Dutchman named Jacob Waltz, who did find gold. Waltz died in 1891, and took his secret with him to his grave. [Ward]

# Painted Rock Petroglyph Site

I f you love ancient rock art like I do, don't miss the ***Painted Rock Petroglyphs***. The amount and variety of designs is mind-boggling. There are over 3800 individual petroglyphs, laboriously pecked onto the surface of 428 boulders. Noble, BLM

The oldest art is of a style known as ***Western Archaic***. These were a group of prehistoric hunter-gatherers who lived in the area between 7500 BC and AD1. They carved geometric and abstract designs with circles, grids, rings, zigzags, and parallel or wavy lines.

The ***Gila Style***, belonging to the Hohokam, is also represented. They contributed artwork between 300 BC and 1450 AD. The Gila Style is known for including animals, insects, humanoids, and plants. Other designs are produced by the O'odham, descendants of the Hohokam.

As I walked around the site, I was amazed by the sheer beauty of the images. The amount of time and energy it must have taken the artists over the centuries to peck the images into the hard rock using only stone tools is unfathomable.

## *How to get to the Painted Rock Petroglyphs:*

The Painted Rock Petroglyph Site is located 30 miles west of the town of Gila Bend, Arizona off of Interstate 8, about 90 miles southwest of Phoenix, Arizona.

# Casa Grande

*C asa Grande Ruins*, meaning "Great House," were named by Father Eusebio Kino in 1694. The main structure is 4 stories high and 60 feet long. It's made of a material called caliche, a mix of sand, clay and limestone. It took 3000 tons of the mixture to build the great house. Over 600 large logs, transported from 50 miles away, supported the roof. Construction was completed in 1350 AD. <sup>Noble, NPS</sup>

The Hohokam lived in the area from 1500 to 550 years ago. They built vast canal systems for irrigation, ballcourts, platforms, and plazas, all surrounded by walls. They traded with Mexico for Macaws, mirrors and copper bells, and were known for their red-on-buff pottery.

When missionaries arrived in 1694, the great house was in ruins. In 1892, it became the country's first archaeological reserve. The walls face the points of the compass and a circular hole in the upper west wall aligns with the setting sun at the summer solstice. Other openings align with the sun and moon at certain times.

The ***Casa Grande Museum*** contains beautiful examples of jewelry
and distinctive pottery.

## *How to get to Casa Grande:*

The Casa Grande ruins are midway between Phoenix and Tucson, 1 mile
north of the town of Coolidge, off Hwy 87.

## *A word about the Anza Expedition:*

Juan Batista de Anza left Mexico in 1775 to explore and colonize the area
known as Alta California. The group included over 30 soldiers, their families, and 1000 livestock. They traveled along the Santa Cruz River Valley,
camping near Casa Grande.

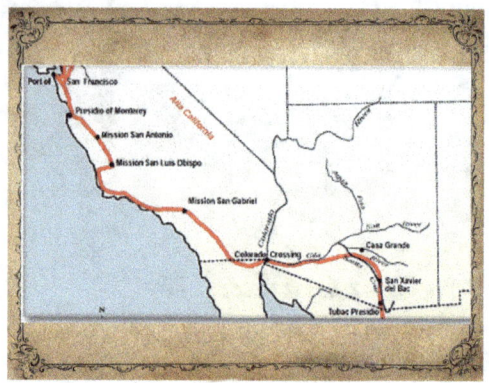

Anza visited Casa Grande on his way to California. He carefully measured and recorded the ruins in his diary before moving on. The Anza Expedition arrived at Mission San Gabriel on January 4, 1776, and later arrived at Monterey on March 10th. Anza continued on to San Francisco Bay and chose a site for their presidio near today's Golden Gate Bridge.

# Besh Ba Gowah

**Besh Ba Gowah**, meaning "place of metal" in Apache, is a sprawling complex of 200 rooms, located in Globe, Arizona. It was built and inhabited by the Salado people from 1225 AD to 1400 AD.

Besh Ba Gowah is a spectacular archaeological park, and unique because there are many interiors with artifacts lying as if they were left there yesterday.

Underneath the ruins there is a much older, prehistoric Hohokam village.
Noble

Don't miss the **Besh Ba Gowah museum** with its fine collection of beautiful black-on-white pottery, textile fragments, spindle whorls, and jewelry.

## *How to get to Besh Ba Gowah:*

Besh Ba Gowah is in Globe, Arizona, 87 miles east of Phoenix.

# Southwestern
# Arizona

# Yuma Territorial Prison

*T*he *Yuma Territorial Prison*, in Yuma, Arizona, was open from 1876 to 1909, and housed a total of 3069 men, women, and children inmates. Yuma Territorial Prison

When you enter the Yuma Territorial Prison, the first structure you see is the imposing **guard tower**, which started out as a water tank. A platform and roof were built over the water tank, and it became the guard tower.

As you walk through the prison, you will see dark, gloomy cell blocks, a potent reminder of how depressing life must have been for incarcerated people.

There is a "dark cell" which is nothing more than an inky black hole where inmates were placed in solitary confinement.

The prison has an excellent **museum**, with a large amount of fascinating artifacts including a variety of hand-crafted items made by inmates. The artistic examples ranged from horse-hair items to beautiful wood inlaid boxes.

The museum and other areas of the prison do an excellent job of telling the life stories of the inmates, through displays and photos.

One of the most desolate areas of the prison is the **prison cemetery**. The graves are marked by piles of rocks, but there are no names to show who they were.

## *How to get to Yuma Territorial Prison:*

Yuma is in the far southwest corner of Arizona, next to California and just north of the Mexican border.

## *A word about hanging:*

Before an inmate was hung, the inmate was weighed.  A sandbag was filled to about the same weight as the inmate. Then, the sandbag was used in an experiment to find out the correct length of rope. The goal was for the inmate to die quickly. If the rope was too long, the inmate could be decapitated. If the rope was too short,

the inmate would slowly strangle to death. If the rope length was "just right" the inmate would die quickly, with a broken neck. Once the right length of rope was found, the execution was ready. The inmate was led up the stairs of the scaffold, blindfolded, with arms and legs tied. The noose was placed around the neck, a trapdoor was sprung, and the inmate fell through the opening to a quick death.

# Southeastern Arizona

# Tucson

*T*ucson is a very walkable, wonderful historic city with lots to see. For shoppers, it has some fascinating artisan markets. For those who like a fine meal, there are lots of great restaurants and open-air food courts to sample. Tucson also has a wide selection of historic sites, making it a very worthwhile stop for history-lovers like me.

Tucson began its life on August 20, 1775, when it was declared a royal presidio of Spain by Hugo O'Conor, an Irishman serving in the Spanish army. The town gained independence from Spain and became a part of Mexico, flying the Mexican flag from 1821 to 1854. Tucson became part of the United States in 1854, and it was tak-

en over by the military in 1856. It didn't take long for gold seekers to come to Tucson. Tucson Presidio Trust for Historic Preservation

Tucson's Main Avenue was once the Calle Real, the royal road which led From Mexico's northern territories, including Tucson, all the way to Mexico City. You can pick up an informative brochure outlining the historic walking tour, known as the **Turquoise Trail**, available at the Art Museum or the Presidio Museum.

The ***Presidio***, originally known as the
Presidio San Agustin, was a military
fort founded by the Irishman Lieu-
tenant Colonel Hugo O'Conor serving in the Spanish Army. The Presidio
had two 20-foot high defensive tow-
ers in the corners, and 10-foot high
walls around the complex. The current Presidio fort is a reconstruction,

but the original 1775 wall foundations still remain.

There are other famous historical
structures to see in Tucson, including
***La Casa Cordova*** which contains
sections of one of the oldest structures
in Tucson. The house was built in
1854, with four rooms added in 1879.

Also worth a stop is the ***Leonardo
Romero House***. The construction
date is unknown, but it was lived in
by Leonardo Romero in 1868. Part of
the house lies along the Presidio wall,
completed in 1783.

Don't miss a visit to the ***Arizona State Museum*** in Tucson. The museum contains a large collection of beautiful pottery, basketry, kachina dolls, and a snowshoe dated between 1450 BC and 1300 BC.

My favorite artifacts within the museum are a pair of split twig animal figures which are 3000 to 4000 years old.

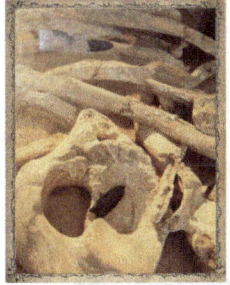

Don't miss the mammoth remains from 13,000 years ago. An arrow point still lies within the remains. The poor animal died of his wounds but wasn't found or eaten by the people who killed him.

Another fascinating Tucson location is the **Hotel Congress**, built in 1919. The interior of the hotel is particularly elegant, with intricate art deco designs and a warm, welcoming atmosphere.

Historically, it's famous for being the spot where John Dillinger and his cohorts were caught in 1934. As the story goes, a fire broke out in the hotel, and Dillinger paid some firemen to carry his bags outside. The firemen wondered why the bags were so heavy. It was because they contained submachine guns and bullet proof vests. The firemen didn't open the bags in spite of the weight, but Dillinger and his gang were recognized from a True Detective mystery magazine.

The old Tucson railroad depot makes a nice peaceful stop on your walk. You can enjoy old wagons and a bit of shade.

It's famous historically because it was where Wyatt Earp and Doc Holliday shot Frank Stilwell, one of the remaining members of the Cowboys, back in 1882. There is a statue at the depot commemorating the event.

## How to get to Tucson:

Tucson is located 118 miles southeast of Phoenix.

# Mission San Xavier Del Bac

***M**ission San Xavier Del Bac* sparkles like a diamond in the desert. It was founded by Jesuit missionary Father Eusebio Kino in 1692, and later rebuilt because of earthquake damage.

Construction on the current church began in 1783, and was completed in 1797. Balfour, Finch

There are at least two priests buried here, including the oldest, Balthazar Carillo, who died in 1795, and Narcissus Gutierrez, who died in 1821.

The ***Mission Museum*** contains
early manuscripts from the 18th cen-
tury, beautifully illuminated, and to-
kens known as milagros, which were
said to heal the sick.

## *How to get to Mission San Xavier del Bac:*

Mission San Xavier del Bac is located about 10 miles south of Tucson.

## *Profiles in history:*

***Father Eusebio Francisco Kino*** was born in Northern Italy in 1645 and
was educated in Bavaria and Austria. He was an astronomer, and cartogra-
pher and first mapped the area known as Pimeria Alta, or the upper lands
of the Pima.

He proved that Baja California was a peninsula and not an island, and he introduced new crops like wheat and domesticated animals including cattle and sheep. He traveled through unknown deserts, valleys and mountain ranges to establish missions in Northern Mexico and southern Arizona. Father Kino died in 1711.

# Tumacacori

***T**umacacori Mission* was established in 1691 in the area known as
New Spain. Father Eusebio Francisco Kino began Tumacacori, the

first mission in what is now Arizona. The O'odham, Yaqui, and Apache met with Jesuit and Franciscan missionaries, settlers, and soldiers at this site.

In 1751 a group of O'odham killed two priests and over 100 Spanish settlers in what was known as the Pima Uprising. After the violence, the first church was completed in 1756. In 1767 King Charles III of Spain banished the Jesuits, and the Franciscans took over the mission. A combination of Apache raids, lack of money, and

lack of government support led to the mission being abandoned.

The current church was completed between 1800 and 1822. A protective Presidio was then built at Tubac 3 miles north. After the Mexican American War, independent Mexico forced all Spanish-born citizens out of the country. Tumacacori's last priest left in 1828.

The columns at the front of the church were originally painted red, with capitals that were yellow with black markings. The style was Egyptian, brought from the Moors in Spain.

The statue niches inside the church were painted blue, with a scallop shell motif to symbolize St. James, the patron saint of Spain. The church contains a *sacristy, baptistery, and main sanctuary*.

The grounds of Tumacacori are beautiful, peaceful, and quiet. It's difficult to believe there was ever any violence here.

The site of the original cemetery is unknown, and contains over 500 burials beginning in 1755. The **new cemetery** contains 36 burials from the years 1822 to 1825, with the last modern burial in 1916. [NPS]

The **museum** contains an amazing collection of artifacts, including a communion wafer press with the Jesuit seal, crucifixes, and statuary.

## *How to get to Tumacacori Mission:*

The Tumacacori Mission is 45 miles south of Tucson.

## *Voices from the past:*

*"These died: Cristobal, father of the captain. He died of the vomit; Rosa died of the yellow vomit; Eusebio died of the same; Juan died of the urine detention; Juanico, first son of the captain, died of throat inflammation."* **Jose de Torres Perea, December, 1743.**

*"In this month and that of April and May...37 children died of this same smallpox epidemic."* **Francisco Xavier Pauer, March, 1764.**

# Fairbank

*F*airbank Historic Townsite is one of my favorite ghost towns, and it is often overlooked by tourists on their way to Tombstone.

Fairbank is a rewarding stop and when I visited, I was able to walk around, completely alone. The first thing that I noticed was the complete stillness of the place. There are only a few buildings, but the history of Fairbank and how it relates to Tombstone is remarkable.

Fairbank was founded in 1882 and was named for a Chicago investor named Nathaniel Fairbank. That's Fairbank, with no "s". It started as a stagecoach stop. Back in the day, a ride on a stage from Fairbank to Tombstone cost $1.50.

Later Fairbank became the railroad depot for Tombstone. The small town boasted a restaurant serving only the finest food, including fresh oysters, all brought in by train. Fairbank also had a bar, a post office, several businesses, a jail, and a school. Many of the famous people of Tombstone, including the Earps, the Cowboys, and others walked the streets of Fairbank. The town was also the scene of a famous train robbery in 1900, carried out by members of Three-finger Jack Dunlap's gang. San Pedro Riparian Natural Conservation Area

My favorite spot in Fairbank is the *cemetery*. You begin walking down a narrow dirt path which turns into an even narrower, crumbling path climbing the steep hill above town. The path circles upward several times until you reach the top, and you can see the entire valley. I wondered at the time how many residents had

climbed this hill to bury their dead. Funerals back in the day must have been strenuous events for the townsfolk of Fairbank.

The cemetery is perched on the very top of the hill, giving you a feeling of being next to God. There are many aged, broken wooden markers, making it impossible to know who is buried beneath them. There are a few sad graves of little children, with small, weathered toys scattered on top of them.

## *How to get to Fairbank:*

Fairbank is 10 miles west of Tombstone, off of Hwy 82.

# Tombstone

**T**ombstone may seem a bit touristy, but that is part of its charm. The streets are lined with historic locations marked by metal plaques, including where Virgil Earp was ambushed and seriously injured on December 28, 1881. You can easily lose yourself strolling down its dusty streets and taking in a historic re-enactment, but there is more to this town. A lot more.

Tombstone received its name from Ed Schieffelin, who began prospecting there in 1877. There are two stories about how the town got its name. One story involves his silver claim being near a grave site. For the second story, see profiles in history, below. By 1881, Tombstone had reached its peak population of 10,000.  Arizona State Parks and Trails

I began my tour of Tombstone at the *Courthouse*, built in 1882. You can see a fascinating collection of artifacts including Wyatt Earp's razor and the bar where the Earps and Doc Holliday had a drink before heading out to the OK Corral.

When in Tombstone, you must visit the **OK Corral**. It's infamous because of a gunfight between the Earps and Doc Holliday, versus the Clantons and McLaury's. The Corral has a small **museum** which contains a hearse with an old embalming kit inside and memorabilia from the Tombstone movie, starring Kurt Russell and Val Kilmer.

When you walk outside, you will see animatronic figures, forever re-enacting the gunfight, old vehicles, a prostitute's crib, and an old photographic studio. OK Corral Museum

My favorite spot to visit in Tombstone is the **Bird Cage Theatre**. The site of the Birdcage was bought for $600 in 1880, and the theater itself opened on December 23, 1881. It didn't take long for the Birdcage to become the hot spot in town. It was in full swing in 1881 through 1889, and boasts 16 gunfights, 140 bullet holes, and 26 violent deaths that happened there.

The Birdcage Theater is named for the 14 birdcage compartments, where patrons could enjoy the services of the ladies. Birdcage Theatre

There is a famous painting still hanging in the Birdcage, known as Fatima, and it has bullet holes and a knife slash to mark some of the events in the theater.

There are several historic areas in the Bird Cage, including where Johnny Ringo and Doc Holliday had their famous duel, and the table at which Doc Holliday dealt and played faro.

The Birdcage contains a large and fascinating collection of artifacts including the original hand-painted stage. My favorite item in the collection is a hearse, called the Black Moriah. It's trimmed in gold and silver and worth at least 2 million dollars.

There is a poker room underneath the stage, where the longest poker game in history was held. The game lasted for 8 years, 5 months and 3 days, with a minimum buy in of $1000. There is a bordello in the basement too. The room at the end is where Wyatt Earp met his mistress Josephine Marcus.

Another of my favorite sights to visit in Tombstone is the ***Boothill Graveyard***. Boothill contains over 250 graves of people, many of which are unknown. The tenants of Boothill died from every cause imaginable, including mining accidents, illnesses like scarlet fever and pneu-

monia, suicide, hanging, shooting, murder, poisoning, and Indian killings.

You will receive an informative guide as to who is buried in Boothill when you pay for admission.

Among the more interesting graves are:

***Charles Helm***, 1882,  who was shot over a disagreement on how cattle should be driven

***Billy Clanton, Frank, and Tom McClaury***, shot by the Earps and Doc Holliday

***Margarita***, a saloon girl who fought with Gold dollar, another dance hall girl, over a man. Gold Dollar stabbed her to death.

***John Heath***, hanged from a tele-graph pole in 1884.

***Mrs. Stump***, who died during childbirth when a doctor adminis-tered an overdose of chloroform

**Dutch Annie**, queen of the red-light district

**George Johnson**, who was hung by mistake for buying a stolen horse

**Marshall White**, who was shot by Curly Bill in 1880 near the Bird Cage

**Lester Moore**, a Wells Fargo agent who died in a dispute over a package. He received "four slugs from a .44, No Les, No More."

**Hancock**, shot in 1879 by Johnny Ringo because he talked badly about a woman

**Two Chinese**, who died of leprosy

**China Mary**, who ruled China-town, and supplied opium and prostitutes to the men of the Tombstone. Her ghost is said to walk the cemetery, wearing a red dress. Boothill Graveyard

### *How to get to Tombstone:*

Tombstone is in southeastern Arizona, 70 miles southeast of Tucson off of Hwy 10.

### *A word about Boothill Cemeteries:*

The term "died with their boots on" began in 1878 and refers to death by murder, or from the result of a criminal act. When they "died with their boots off" it means death from natural causes.

### *Profiles in history:*

***Ed Schieffelin***, the founder of Tombstone, Arizona was a courageous man who began prospecting at the age of 12. Braving attacks by hostile Indians, he came into the Tombstone area looking for silver in 1877. He was warned by members of nearby Camp Huachuca that all he would find was his own tombstone.

After working diligently for three years, Schieffelin was anxious to see other parts of the country, so in 1880, he was offered $300,000 for his claims, which he accepted. He continued to travel across the West for the rest of his life, dying in Oregon in 1897.

It was Schieffelin's wish to be buried in the desert, close to Tombstone, where he now rests:

*"It is my wish, if convenient, to be buried in the dress of a prospector, my old pick and canteen with me, on top of the granite hills about three miles westerly from the city of Tombstone, Arizona, and that a monument such as prospectors build when locating a mining claim be built over my grave...under no circumstances do I want to be buried in a graveyard or cemetery."*

## A moment in time:

The **gunfight at the OK (Old Kindersley) Corral**, was not actually in the OK Corral. The story behind the OK Corral began when cattle rustlers named the Cowboys, led by Curly Bill Brocus and Johnny Ringo, along with another group, the McLaury brothers, controlled all of the access to water and began stealing cattle. The Cowboys didn't stop with just cattle. They committed the first Wells Fargo robbery in 1879. The Cowboys were protected by a corrupt sheriff named John Behan.

Lawmen Wyatt and Virgil Earp, along with their brother Morgan, were residents of Tombstone. On October 25, 1881, Ike Clanton, a member of the Cowboys, came into town, became very drunk and threatened to kill the Earps and their friend, Doc Holliday.

The next morning, on October 26, 1881, Ike Clanton was joined by his Brother Billy, Frank and Tom McLaury and Billy Claiborne.

Wyatt, Virgil, and Morgan Earp began to walk down the street to arrest the Clantons and their friends for violating the town's firearms ordinance. The Earps were joined by Doc Holliday.

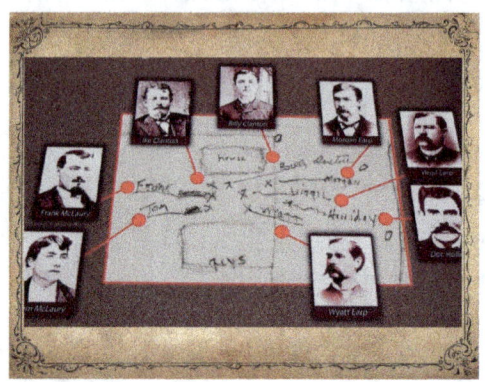

The cowboys waited in an open lot near Fremont street. The Earps confronted the Cowboys. Each side fired 17 shots, and at the end Frank and Tom McLaury and Billy Clanton were dead, Virgil, Morgan, and Doc were injured, only Wyatt remained unhurt. The whole incident took only 30 seconds. The photo above is a map of the gunfight, drawn by Wyatt Earp.
OK Corral Museum

## *Voices from the past:*

*"I found him a loyal friend and good company. He was a dentist whom necessity had made a gambler; a gentleman whom disease had made a vagabond; a philosopher whom life had made a caustic wit; a long, lean blonde fellow nearly dead with consumption and at the same time the most skillful gambler and nerviest, speediest, dead-*

*liest man with a six-gun I ever knew."* **Wyatt Earp on his friend, Doc Holliday.**

## *Ghost story:*

Ghostly happenings in the Birdcage involve the hat on Wyatt Earp's statue being thrown about the room. As the story goes, the statue was in an area where the Clanton gang frequently sat. The statue was moved, and the hat throwing suddenly stopped.

Another frequent ghost at the Birdcage is the **"Lady in White"**, a woman that appears in a white dress and white bonnet. The ghost is believed to be Carmelita Gimenes, a singer at the Birdcage who committed suicide by poisoning herself with rat poison. [Polston]

I was lucky enough to photograph a "ghost" in one of the birdcages. When you visit, don't forget to ask the front desk about ghosts. A staff member showed me a collection of several ghostly photographs, including a ghost dog.

## Ghost story:

*John Wesley Heath* was the mastermind of a robbery known as the "Bisbee Massacre" in which several citizens including a pregnant woman and a deputy were shot and killed. Heath didn't do any of the killing, and claimed to know nothing about the killings, but he was sentenced to life in prison at the Yuma Territorial Prison.

The citizens gathered in Tombstone and mobbed the jail where Heath was being held. They took Heath on Feb 22, 1884, blindfolded him, and hung him from a telephone pole at First and Toughnut street. An apparition, believed to be the ghost of John Wesley

Heath has been seen walking at night
down Toughnut street. [Polston]

## *A word about prostitutes:*

Prostitutes, also known as "sporting girls," "soiled doves," and several other names, typically charged $10 per session, or  $25 for an overnight rendezvous. They had one day a week off, and had to bathe at least 3 times each week.

One famous Tombstone madam named Dutch Annie, gave aid and comfort to the unfortunate in town. When Dutch Annie died, over 1000 buggies followed her corpse to the cemetery.

# Chiricahua
# Mountains

*The Chiricahua Mountains* are a spectacularly beautiful place to camp, with some history as well. Neil and Emma Erickson came here from Sweden and married in 1887. They homesteaded in the Chiricahuas, establishing the *Faraway Ranch* in 1886, one of the first permanent dwellings here. The ranch was named by Lillian Erickson because it was "God-awful far away from everything."

The ranch is still here, and there is a small *cemetery* where most of the Erickson family members are buried. The Ericksons were largely responsible for the Chiricahua National Monument being established in 1924.

Chiricahua Mountains

The Chiricahua Apache called the area "The Land of Standing-Up Rocks" because of the uniquely stunning upright rock formations known as the *Pinnacles*.

As you travel through the monument, you will come upon the **Stafford Cabin**, built by Ja Hu Stafford in 1880. Originally the cabin had only one room and a dirt floor. The cabin was later purchased to become a guest house for the Faraway Ranch.

## *How to get to the Chiricahua Mountains:*

The Chiricahua National Monument is  located near Wilcox, Arizona. From Wilcox, take Hwy. 186 for 32 miles, and turn left onto Hwy. 181. Go 4 miles to the entrance to the monument.

# Favorite Places to Camp

*N**avajo National Monument** offers spectacular cliff dwellings and 2 campgrounds, the Sunset View and Canyon View campgrounds, both of which have free camping on a first come, first serve basis. You can camp up to 7 days, and there are no hookups for RVs.

***Bonita Canyon Campground*** in the Chiricahua Mountains offers wonderful rock formations, hiking trails, and 26 campsites available by reservation at ***Recreation.gov***. Picnic tables and water are available.

***Dispersed camping*** is available throughout Arizona, especially around Lake Mead National Recreation Area, Castle Dome, and Yuma . Take plenty of water when camping in the Arizona outback.

# Random Thoughts
## What History Means to Me

First, let me start by sharing with you my opinion of what history isn't. History is not a collection of random dates, names, and places for you to memorize. History is not a dry and uninteresting class you have to pass to graduate.

I believe history is a tangible thing. You can actually *feel* history in the places you go, and the sights you see. I remember walking up to the Acropolis in Athens. I looked down at the well-worn marble steps and wondered about how many ancient philosophers had climbed these very steps, thousands of years ago.

You don't have to go far away to experience the *feeling* of history. If you are lucky enough to live in an old house, you may experience history in your own surroundings. You might say to yourself, *"If only these walls could talk."*

During my travels across the United States, I *felt* history in many, many places. If you travel across the country like I did, you will *feel* the wonderful history of our beautiful country for yourself, and you will never be the same. You will discover what it means to be an American.

## *Why I did it and why you can too:*

I decided to travel across the country by car because I wanted to rediscover America. When I first set out to explore the history of our country, I wanted to find out why America is the greatest country on earth, and what it means to be an American.

The politics of these United States was frightening at the time. Our country was polarized, almost beyond repair. Whether it was Democrats or Republicans, Conservatives, or Liberals, everyone was fighting.

I wanted to rediscover the joy of being an American. I wanted to rediscover our rich history, our unique and wonderful people, our tapestry of multicultural heritage, and our rich natural resources. I thought a road trip by car across eleven western states was a good place to start.

I have a degree in Archaeology, and a passion for all things archaeological. I love history, with a side love of paleontology. It is these three passions that I set my trip agenda around. I set out to discover the archaeological sites, history, and paleontological world of our country.

As I travel and write my books, I get asked all the time, especially by women, "What is it like to travel by yourself? Aren't you scared?" The truth is, I believe everyone should do what I did. It's a wonderful way to discover our country, and to rediscover yourself. The truth is, I'm scared not to travel. Traveling allows you to get to know yourself, in ways not possible when sitting on the couch watching TV.

We tend to spend a lot of our lives tuning out the world and our place within it. When you travel, you are quite literally forced to deal with your own thoughts, emotions, and feelings. You can discover yourself while traveling. You can come to understand what makes you who you are, and how you can perhaps become a better person. Above all, traveling gives you mental clarity to figure out how to live with intent. It's a way to guide your life, not just wait for things to happen.

# Travel Tips & Stuff
## What You Need to Know

### *How to get started:*

P lanning your trip should be one of the most exciting things about it. You want to be spontaneous, but it is also very wise to plan your route, so you can take full advantage of all the time and miles you will invest.

First, decide your passions. If you love airplanes, trains, or old vehicles, plan your trip around that. If you love gardens or architecture, seek that out as the focus of your trip.

Next, read and research areas of the country that will let you enjoy what you are interested in.

Make a list by state and city or town, of what you want to see.

Take your handy road atlas and locate the areas on the pages.

Make a tentative route plan, so you have an idea of where you are going.

*Travel tip:* Avoid trying to plan your trip down to a schedule of days, hours, or minutes. On a road trip, it will be virtually impossible to know where you will be on any given day. If you adhere to a schedule, you are more likely to stress out, and less likely to actually enjoy yourself, which is the whole point.

## *What you need:*

You need to bring along a sense of adventure and a curious mind. You need to ditch the idea of always being on a schedule, and live a little more spontaneously to thoroughly enjoy yourself. Things will happen as you travel, both good things and bad things, and you need to prepare your mind and your soul for day-to-day changes.

So much of our lives are planned out. Between growing up, going to school, finding a career, marriage, kids, or whatever, people have lost much of the ability to be spontaneous. But you must take spontaneity on the trip with you, because you may make detours along the way to see something really spectacular.

### *So, for the practical stuff you need:*

**A great vehicle**-I have a Honda CRV which is fabulous. It's old, a 2004, fully paid for, and will go anywhere. I see humongous RVs on the road, towing a car behind, and all I can think of is, they can't go just anywhere. They are too big. Bad gas mileage, cumbersome to drive, slow, and not agile like my CRV. So, I encourage you, if you want to go car camping and be able to go on remote dirt roads, get an agile vehicle, and Hondas are great.

*Travel tip:* Don't be afraid to do some modifications to your vehicle. I took one of my back seats out. (after watching a YouTube video) I threw in a twin mattress, a bit of drapery, and some netting. I also put some of those little portable light switches on the inside. I jettisoned anything I hadn't used up to that point. Don't be afraid to get rid of unnecessary stuff.

**An awesome camera** that you know inside and out. I use a Nikon and it takes wonderful pictures. Don't skimp on a camera, and don't think a cellphone camera is all you need, because you want the best for your beautiful photos.

**A hot plate warmer**-this little item was indispensable. You need a converter for it so you can plug it in to the cigarette lighter. Place your food inside it, carton and all, and then plug it in. 30 minutes for thawed food, about an hour and a half for frozen food. Boom! You have a hot meal by the time you stop for the night!

**Window shades**-the best ones are magnetic so you just place them against your windows and they cling to them, obscuring the view inside your car.

**Portable cooler with wheels**-another indispensable item that works great and is easy to move around. I use those nifty blue frozen blocks in mine.

**Portable air compressor**-this little gem plugs into your cigarette lighter and will inflate your tires if you have a flat. Fortunately, I haven't had to use this yet.

**Portable battery charger and power bank**-mine comes with battery cables and the power bank, yet once inside the case, it is small enough to put in your glove compartment. This little item, unfortunately, I have had to use, and it saved me.

**Portable generator**-mine came with a small solar panel, so it can be charged with solar or electricity. It has a decent battery life and also doubles as a light for night-time.

**All season clothing**-you never know what different states will bring for weather, so take hot weather and cold weather clothes, and a fair amount of shoes appropriate for hiking, or walking, sandals, and slippers, which are nice at night. Also take along a pair of cheap rubber flip-flops to wear in the public showers you might go into.

**Your own pillows**-I like my own pillows, so I don't wake up with neck cramps, especially after sleeping in the car.

**Sleeping bag and cozy blankets**-you want to stay warm and layering is everything.

**Warm hat, warm socks, and fuzzy jammies** to keep you warm for cold nights sleeping in the car.

**A great road atlas, and great guidebooks**-get one that's easy to read, with great pictures. For a road atlas, just get one that is easy to read.

## *A word about photography:*

Along with a great camera, you need to have a great eye. This is easier than it sounds once you have worked with your camera and are comfortable taking pictures with it. I am not a professional photographer, but I like my pictures and other people do too.

These are my tips for taking great pictures:

- Experiment with taking both horizontal and vertical shots.

- Don't always put the subject of the photo in the middle of the photograph.

- This one is important: pay attention to the foreground, and if possible, have something, a plant or whatever, in the foreground to help give the photo dimension and depth.

- This one is important too: turn around often to see the view you just came from. I do this quite often and some of my best pictures have resulted from when I turned around and took the shot.

You can also take a mental photo. Place an image in your mind that you can call upon later. Use all of your senses to see, hear, smell, and maybe even to taste, what is around you. You have the means to fully experience your surroundings, and that is very important to a traveler. When you take a mental photo, be sure to jot down quick little details about what you saw, heard, smelled, or tasted, so you can jog your memory later.

And last, but not least...don't be posing in front of everything, everywhere, to show that you actually went somewhere. Most people want to see themselves in your photo and be mentally transported there, but they can't if you are there already.

## *To camp or not to camp:*

Car camping is great. I prefer it to sleeping on the cold, hard ground in a tent. I can lock the doors, put my window shades up and be cozy for the night.

That being said, for me there were some do's and don'ts about camp sites. Some people camp in a Walmart parking lot and feel safe. I do not. I believe that if you are in a busy area, you're more likely to be confronted by a nut job who may bother you. Nothing against Walmart.

Same goes for casino parking lots. Many people believe that if they are in a public place, there is less chance of someone bothering them. I don't share this belief. I believe you are safer parked out in the middle of nowhere in the dark. That same nut job who can find you in a parking lot is not about to go driving around on dirt roads to see if anyone is parked there. At least that's my belief. You may not share it,  and that's fine. Park and camp wherever you feel safe.

I don't go for rest areas either because they have a track record of incidents happening to people in rest areas, especially women travelers.

So, where do I camp? In state or national campgrounds, wildlife sanctuaries, or off on a dirt road somewhere, usually out in the middle of nowhere.

There are definitely times when I stay in a motel. I use Hotels.com because I like their stay 10 nights, get 1 night free deal. So, I book a hotel or motel if:

- The weather is too hot or too cold, or too rainy

- I am in a city and plan to stay awhile

- I'm tired of camping, need a shower, or my body hurts

- I need to do laundry

## *A word about safety:*

When you are a woman traveling alone, it's critical to keep a low profile. Don't tell people you are traveling alone, where you are staying, or any other personal information.

I don't go to bars or get drunk. I'm not preaching but you are on your own, in a city or town you've never been to, and you don't know anyone, so it's not the time to lose control of what you are doing. When you are in control, you are better able to decide which people you want to get to know better.

***Travel tip:*** If you feel vulnerable traveling alone, that's OK. Vulnerability is part of passion, and traveling is a passionate thing to do. You can put one of those family stickers on your vehicle to indicate to others that you are not traveling alone, which can help you feel more secure.

## *Maintain your connections:*

When you are traveling alone, there is a definite sense of disconnection. It feels almost like you are the only one in the world, traveling through space and time. That's why it's critical to keep your connections to loved ones active.

Be on Facebook while you are traveling. You may not have internet a lot of the time, or the internet will be poor. Consider paying to have your phone be a hotspot. It's a little bit of money per month, but it's worth it and has saved me from being without internet. I love the convenience of it, and you will too.

Plan your journey around visiting family members or friends you haven't seen for a long time, or people that are good friends. When you see people you know, it will ground you, so you can continue traveling.

Check in by phone with loved ones. They worry about you, and it's good for both of you to stay connected no matter where you are.

Consider traveling with a pet. I started my trip with my beloved 14-year-old sheltie named Sadie. She didn't make it to the end of the trip. I lost her to bladder cancer about four months in. My Sadie was special, and I will never forget my first traveling buddy.

It took me a solid year to decide on getting another dog. I poured over profiles of rescue dogs, looking for a little buddy I could take care of. Best Friends Animal Society in Kanab, Utah, had my perfect match. I now have Rosie, an 8 year-old sheltie that looks just like Sadie and has many of the same mannerisms. Life is good again.

I highly recommend Best Friends Animal Society if you are looking for a pet. They have 3000 acres and house up to 1600 animals at one time including dogs, cats, horses, pigs, and just about everything else. The dedicated people at Best Friends are wonderful both to you, and your potential pet.

***Travel tip:*** One of the easiest and best ways I stay connected while traveling is to offer to take a photo for someone I don't know. Many couples, families, or singles would love to have more pictures of themselves traveling. It's an easy and quick way to have a connection with a fellow traveler, and it's good manners too.

## Practical matters:

You need to have an address to send your mail to. Keep in touch with whomever is nice enough to do this for you.

You will also need to come back occasionally to register your car, vote, go to doctor visits, and take care of any other business. You can't leave it all behind, as tempting as that may be.

## Bad things that happened:

Remember when I said you need to take spontaneity with you on your trip? Well, there were many times when I used my spontaneity skillset.

The government shutdown happened smack dab in the middle of my travels. That meant that all of the National Monuments were closed. I did a lot of driving and circling around.

I also did a lot of circling around trying to avoid natural disasters. I traveled through Paradise, California shortly before a massive fire happened there. I tried to travel through the area again but was pushed out by massive flooding. My latest event was camping in Canyonville, Oregon and waking up to flames creeping down the hillside. That was day one of the Canyonville fire.

Besides being driven out by natural disasters, sometimes I was driven out by rude people. Many times it was centered around my furry traveling companion. I believe there are really only two types of people, those who love animals and those who don't. When people see me walking my beautiful, sweet, elderly dog, they either come up and pet her, or they say something harsh.

One incident was a woman, a total stranger, who came up to me smiling down at Sadie and asked how old she was. I replied, "She is 13 and a half years old." The woman replied very curtly "She needs to be put down." Sadie was walking around, alert, and happy, and yet this woman wanted me to end her life because she was old.

Speaking of animals, several times I came very close to driving into an animal on the road. I can't stress enough how many times this will happen to you, and all I can say is, be alert at all times while you are driving. When you travel a lot of miles, you will get tired, so stop and smell the roses, and try not to drive at night.

### *Good things that happened:*

One of the sheer joys of taking a road trip is the unpredictability of it. You never know what you will see. I am originally from Oregon, and bears are not a common sight. So, while driving high up in the Blue Mountains, I looked over and saw a bear! So exciting! He didn't stay for long, kind of shy, but so cute. I love animals, so to see the rich and wonderful amount of wildlife in our country gladdened my heart.

I met many great people on my trip, from all walks of life. They were a walking, talking advertisement for our beautiful country. I smiled at them, and they smiled back. We are all Americans, and we are all part of the human race. When you meet people across the country, you realize just how important it is to get to know your fellow citizens, and learn more about how they view the world and our country.

I have to give a special shout-out to the many dedicated people, often volunteers, who staff our state and national parks and monuments. They work tirelessly to ensure the health of our natural resources, and help travelers enjoy their visit. The same is true of the many people who staff the museums in small towns and large cities. They enjoy history, like I do, and it shows in their smiles.

Along with wonderful people, I have seen an America that is spectacularly beautiful, with open prairies, majestic mountains, and crystal clear rivers. I have seen a small fraction of the history of our country. I have seen the memorials to the brave people who shaped our country. I have fallen in love with America in a way that was not possible sitting in my living room. People ask me, "would I do it again?" The answer comes easily, "Yes, in a heartbeat."

# Bibliography & Further Reading

*Aztec Ruins*, National Park Service

Balfour, Amy C. *Southwest USA's Best Trips: 32 Amazing Road Trips*. Lonely Planet, 2014.

*Bandelier National Monument Main Loop Trail Guide*, Western National Parks Association

*Boothill Graveyard*, Boothill Graveyard

*Canyon De Chelly*, National Park Service

*Casa Grande Ruins*, National Park Service

*Chaco Culture*, National Park Service

Chino, Conroy. *Petroglyphs of the Southwest: a Puebloan Perspective*. Western National Parks Association, 2012.

Crutchfield, James A. *It Happened in Colorado: Remarkable Events That Shaped History*. TwoDot, 2017.

Diamond, Jared M. *Collapse: How Societies Choose to Fail or Succeed*. Penguin Books, 2011.

Enss, Chris. *Object, Matrimony: the Risky Business of Mail-Order Matchmaking on the Western Frontier*. Globe Pequot Press, 2013.

Enss, Chris. *Tales behind the Tombstones*. Morris Pub., 2007.

Enss, Chris. *The Doctor Wore Petticoats: Women Physicians of the Old West*. TwoDot, 2006.

Eppinga, Jane. *Tombstone*. Arcadia Pub., 2010.

Eppinga, Jane. *Tucson*. Arcadia Publishing, 2015.

*Fairbank Historic Townsite*, San Pedro Riparian Nat. Conservation Area

Finch, etc. al.., Jackie. *Eyewitness Travel USA*. DK Publishing, 2017.

Geissinger, Terri Lynn. *Bodie*. Arcadia Publishing, 2009.

*Guide to the Heritage Sites, Palatki, V Bar V, Honanki*, US Forest Service and Friends of the Forest, 2015.

Hill, William E. *The Oregon Trail, Yesterday and Today: a Brief History and Pictorial Journey along the Wagon Tracks of Pioneers*. Caxton Press, 2014.

*Homolovi State Park*, Arizona State Parks and Trails

Krause, Mariella. *Southwest USA's Best Trips: 32 Amazing Trips*. Lonely Planet, 2014.

Mayo, Matthew P. *Haunted Old West: Phantom Cowboys, Spirit-Filled Saloons, Mystical Mine Camps, and Spectral Indians*. Globe Pequot Press, 2012.

*Meteor Crater Brief History*, Meteor Crater Enterprises

*Montezuma Castle and Tuzigoot*, National Park Service

*Montezuma Well*, National Park Service

Munn, Debra D. *Wyoming Ghost Stories: Eerie True Tales*. Riverbend, 2008.

*Navajo National Monument*, National Park Service

Noble, David Grant. *Ancient Ruins and Rock Art of the Southwest: an Archaeological Guide*. Taylor Trade Publishing, 2015.

Noble, David Grant. *Ancient Ruins of the Southwest: an Archaeological Guide*. Northland Pub., 2000.

*OK Corral Guide Map*, OK Corral Museum

*The Old Birdcage Theatre*, Birdcage Theatre

*Old Spanish Trail*, Bureau of Land Management, 2012.

*Painted Rock Petrolglyph Site*, Bureau of Land Management

Pascoe, Jill. *Haunted Arizona*. Irongate Press, 2008.

*Pecos*, National Park Service

Polston, Cody. *Haunted Tombstone*. Haunted America, 2018.

Rutter, Michael. *Bedside Book of Bad Girls: Outlaw Women of the American West*. Farcountry Press, 2008.

*Salinas Pueblo Missions*, National Park Service

Scott, Robert. *Plain Enemies: Best True Stories of the Frontier West*. Caxton Printers, 1995.

*Tombstone Courthouse*, Arizona State Parks and Trails

*Tonto*, National Park Service

*Tumacacori*, National Park Service

*Tumacacori: In the Footprints of the Past*, National Park Service, 2013.

*The Turquoise Trail*, Tucson Presidio Trust for Historic Preservation, 2018.

*Visitor Guide to Kinishba*, John Welch, Karl Hoerig, Stephen Grede, White Mountain Apache Tribe, 2016.

*Walnut Canyon*, National Park Service

Ward, Bob. *True Story of Superstition Mountains: Ripples of Lost Echos*. Tract Evangelistic Crusade, 1990.

*Yuma Territorial Prison*, Yuma Territorial Prison Map

# Index

## Referenced by Sections

### A

# D

# E

# F

# N

# O

# T

# About the Author

***Julie Bettendorf*** is a world traveler with a degree in archaeology and a background in history. She has traveled extensively throughout Egypt, Central America, South America, Europe, and the United Kingdom, visiting archaeological and historical sites all along the way.

Currently, Julie is traveling around the US visiting ghost towns, ancient rock art sites, and archaeological wonders as part of research for her ongoing historical travel series entitled Wandering Woman. Wandering Woman is a set of state-by-state guides, full of photographs, historical anecdotes, and unique tips to help other women travel and explore solo across the US by car. Julie enjoys writing freelance blogs, traveling frequently with her two adult children, and hiking outdoors with her faithful dog companion Rosie.

# Also by Julie Bettendorf

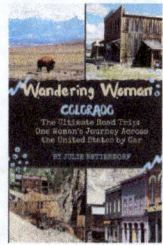

*Wandering Woman: Arizona* is the eighth book in the *Wandering Woman Travel Series*. The first seven books *Wandering Woman: Montana*, *Utah*, *Nevada*, *Colorado*, *Washington*, *Oregon, and Wandering Woman: Idaho* are available in ebook and paperback.

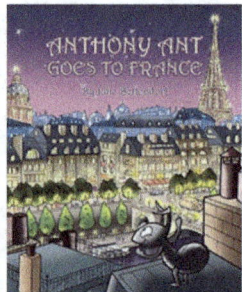

Julie has published two children's books in an ongoing, beautifully illustrated travel series entitled ***Anthony Ant Goes to France*** and ***Anthony Ant Goes to Egypt.***

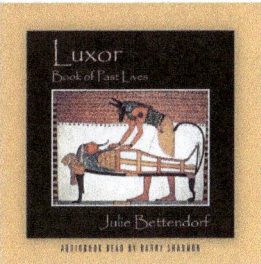

She has also published a work of historical fiction entitled ***Luxor: Book of Past Lives*** which has recently been released as an audiobook, read by renowned narrator Barry Shannon.